Original title:
Icicles and Snowdrifts

Copyright © 2024 Creative Arts Management OÜ
All rights reserved.

Author: Maxwell Donovan
ISBN HARDBACK: 978-9916-94-580-3
ISBN PAPERBACK: 978-9916-94-581-0

Frosted Haze

On windows bright, a chilly sprint,
The dog slid past, forgot to print.
With every snowball, laughter flies,
As mittens launch from tiny ties.

A hot cocoa dare, we toast and sip,
But then a marshmallow takes a dip.
With frosty breath, we plot and scheme,
To build a scowl—a snowman's dream!

The Calm After the Flurry

The world is blank, a frosted sheet,
Yet squirrelly critters dance on feet.
A slide of sleet, a tumble down,
As winter wears its glistening crown.

We search for boots, but find a shoe,
The snowman's carrot, borrowed too.
Around the trees, the laughter swells,
As snowflakes ring their tiny bells.

A Symphony of Snow

The orchestra plays, each flake a sound,
While snowflakes twirl and swirl around.
We grab our hats, it's time to play,
With frosty tunes that steal the day.

A snow fort built, a fortress grand,
And snowballs launched by eager hand.
But someone trips, a slip, a dance,
In frosted fun, we take a chance!

Frosty Whispers

The whispers drift on chilly air,
With laughter masked behind a stare.
A snowman's grin, a silly grin,
As snowplows grunt and begin to spin.

We take a ride on sleds with glee,
But puddles hide with sneak and spree.
With puddles splashed, we shake and shout,
And dance around—what's winter about?

The Blanket of Winter

A cozy quilt of chilly white,
It wraps the world both day and night.
Snowmen wobble, hats askew,
While children giggle, shouting 'Boo!'

The ground is slick, watch your step,
With every twist, a little prep.
But as we tumble in delight,
We laugh and roll, our hearts so light.

Frosty Luminescence

Twinkling lights on frozen streams,
Reflecting all our winter dreams.
The squirrels slide, they think they're sleek,
While plump old pigeons play hide and seek.

A snowball fight turns into war,
With laughter echoing more and more.
As frosty breath fills up the air,
The neighbors join, caught unaware.

Specters of the Cold

Ghostly forms in fluffy coats,
Sliding past like laughing boats.
With mismatched gloves and socks too bright,
We prance like ghosts in the pale moonlight.

Chattering teeth and rosy noses,
Winter's breath, how it dozes.
With every sneeze, a joke unwinds,
Who knew the chill made us so kind?

A Dusting of Dreams

Sprinkles of white on rooftops lay,
Transforming homes into shades of play.
Each puff of snow, a laughing joker,
As we tumble down, a swoosh, a choker!

The trees stand tall, in a fluffy gown,
While the lonely cat wears a snowy crown.
In this fantasy of fluff so bright,
We dance in dreams, till morning light.

Beneath the Blanket of Snow

The ground is white, oh what a sight,
Little feet dance, in pure delight.
Snowflakes fall, a chilly call,
But who needs warmth when you can sprawl?

Lumpy throws made quite the hill,
Sledding down gives quite the thrill.
With icy cheeks and laughter bright,
We'll rule this winter, oh what a plight!

Carved Memories in the Frost

A snowy canvas on which we play,
With frozen toes, we shout hooray!
Artistry comes from a little shove,
What a masterpiece, we might just love!

Frosty mittens are quite a sight,
As snowballs fly, oh what a fight!
Giggles echo through the air,
Chasing fun without a care.

A Tapestry of Crystal Silence

Blankets of fluff, we snuggle and roll,
What's that in the air? A snowman goal!
With a carrot nose and buttons galore,
He might just dance if we ask for more!

Frosty fingers wrapped in greed,
Softly landing as they plead.
And in the night, we take our stand,
A snowy battle, oh isn't it grand?

Frozen Tendrils

Nature's fingers, stretched so wide,
Catching laughter as we slide.
A sprinkle here, a splash there,
Who knew that winter had a flare?

The branches droop, but spirits rise,
With snowmen grinning, oh what a prize!
The air is crisp, the jokes go fast,
In a wintry world that's far from last.

Arctic Shadows Beneath the Moon

In a land where penguins waddle with grace,
Snowmen gossip, stuck in one place.
Noses made of carrots, hats crooked to fit,
They laugh at the frosty, unwelcome skit.

Frosty feet dance on slippery ground,
While polar bears chuckle, no sound can be found.
Chasing seals wearing hats, a unique fashion,
They trip on the frozen, it's quite the distraction.

Glittering Prisms of the Cold

The frost sparkles bright like confetti in flight,
Snowflakes tickle noses, a magical sight.
Snowball fights break out like an ice-bound brawl,
Each throw a chance for a wintery fall.

The snowman called Fred confesses his dreams,
To join in the races on overstuffed beams.
He imagines a sleigh with a rocket-blast twist,
But forgets that he'd melt – oh, how he's missed!

Whispered Secrets in White

The trees wear a blanket, fluffy and light,
While squirrels play hide and seek in delight.
They snicker and chatter about winter's grand show,
Plotting a prank on the dog down below.

Winter invites all the critters to play,
As snowflakes wear glasses in a dazzling display.
They tumble and spin, creating great mirth,
As raccoons make snow angels, proving their worth.

Frigid Blossoms on the Branches

The branches hang low with their frozen charms,
An owl on a perch, sounding alarm.
He jokes with the wind, how chilly it feels,
While snowmen dream big, sharing their meals.

A prancing hare hops, too much energy shown,
In pajamas of snow, that's wildly his own.
He trips on a branch and slips with a squeak,
Creating a laughter-filled, wintery week.

Moonlit Snowflakes

Beneath the moon's bright glow, they dance,
A frozen ballet, a lacy trance.
They twinkle and spin, with a wink so sly,
Who knew cold could be so spry?

A snowball flies, but not too far,
It hits a tree, oh what a star!
It clings and dangles, oh so bold,
A frosty prank that never gets old.

Chilled Echoes

The wind whispers secrets, a chilly jest,
As snowmen giggle, they're feeling blessed.
One lost a carrot, it rolls away,
"Hey! Come back!" they shout, in a frosty play.

Slipping and sliding on icy trails,
Laughter erupts, the good mood prevails.
With every tumble, a snowflake's cheer,
Winter's a circus; let's hold dear!

Frost-Patterned Dreams

A blanket of white, so fluffily bright,
Where penguins play in the frosty light.
Chasing each other, they slide with grace,
It's a penguin party, in this chilly place!

But wait, what's that? A snowman's hat?
"Is it mine?" "No, no, it's a cat!"
With giggles and purrs, they all convene,
In winter's theater, they're quite the scene.

Glistening Landscapes

The world is a canvas, frosty and bright,
Where squirrels wear boots, what a hilarious sight!
They leap on the snow, with flair and style,
As winter chuckles and grins all the while.

A snowball fight erupts with a cheer,
"Gotcha!" "Missed me!" so loud and clear.
With laughter ringing, and spirits high,
This winter wonderland sure knows how to fly!

Frosted Light

The sun peeks out and gives a grin,
It tells the snowman, "Let's begin!"
With carrot noses, bright and bold,
They dance around, but still, they're cold.

A mistletoe hangs overhead,
While snowballs fly, they aim for heads!
The laughter rings through frosty air,
As hats go flying everywhere!

A polar bear slips on a patch,
Grabs a penguin, thinks he's a catch!
With flippers flailing, they both crash,
In a snowy pile, what a splash!

With puffs of breath, they blow little clouds,
While the pine trees wear their snowy shrouds.
Amidst the fun, the chill is quite clear,
But who can fuss when there's such cheer?

Silent Transformations

The silent night transforms the ground,
Where jolly snowmen dance around.
With icy hats and scarves that sway,
They shimmy, twist in wild ballet.

A dog comes by, slips with a yelp,
In a snowy drift, he digs for help.
While children giggle, rolling near,
The pup shakes off, his mood still cheer!

A snowflake lands upon a nose,
With teasing friends, he strikes a pose!
"Look at me! I'm frost, I'm flair!"
But down he tumbles, unaware!

The evening fades, and stars appear,
While snowmen plot and share a beer.
They toast to nights so chilly and bright,
As snowflakes twirl, it feels just right!

Frozen Reverie

In the garden, a snow cat lies,
With frosted paws and sleepy eyes.
He dreams of chasing winter mice,
While deer on skates slide not so nice.

A rabbit hops, all fluffy and white,
Skidding backward with all its might.
It tries to slide, but goes astray,
A tumble here, then off to play!

Chirps of birds sound from afar,
While snowmen bling with a broken car.
Their ride won't budge, it seems stuck fast,
Yet they all chuckle, having a blast!

The frozen trees, they crack and creak,
As creatures trample, hide, and peek.
In joyful chaos, laughter rings,
While winter smiles and brings its things!

Icy Sequences

A snowball fight breaks out in glee,
With slippery socks and falling spree.
One glance away, and oh dear me!
A face full of frost, how can this be?

The squirrels jump from branch to branch,
With ice skates on, they take a chance.
A crowd of owls watches in awe,
As one goes airborne, causing a flaw.

The winter sun shines bright and bold,
Lifting spirits from the cold.
With snowflakes swirling as they play,
They giggle loud, not far away!

As night descends, they gather tight,
To share their tales of snowy delight.
With rosy cheeks and joyous face,
They'll carry memories to embrace!

Frost-Kissed Shadows

A chilly breeze plays tag with my nose,
As frosty figures dance in silly rows.
They waddle and wobble, it's quite a sight,
Snowmen with hats that tip left and right.

A squirrel in a vest tries to impress,
While my frozen feet just want to rest.
I slip on ice, do the wintery slide,
Laughing at ghosts that tumble and glide.

The Weight of Stillness

Everything wraps in a soft, white hug,
Except for the snowman, who's pulled a rug.
With carrot nose stuck in a mini fight,
He argues with kids 'til they lose their sight.

The crunch of footsteps feels quite profound,
While laughter echoes in the winter ground.
A dog rolls crazy, a snowball to chase,
And I'm left laughing 'til I lose my grace.

Silvered Branches

Trees adorned in sparkles, where did they shop?
Nature's own glitter, a wintery prop.
Birds perched like jewels, they fluff and they fuss,
Puffing their chests like fine old bus.

A branch bends low, heavy with surprise,
As a clumsy elf dances, oh my, oh my!
They slip and they slide, the snow plays its tune,
While I sip hot cocoa, under the moon.

A Tapestry of Snow

A blanket lays thick, covering each spot,
While the neighbors' pets plot a snowball plot.
Rabbits in boots hop with casual flair,
As they dodge all the snowflakes floating in air.

With every soft flake, giggles arise,
As sisters in mittens throw friendly pies.
The cold can't defeat such warm, silly glee,
In this wintry land, where we're all set free.

Beneath the Icy Surface

Under the frosty cover,
A penguin slips and falls,
He shouts, "What is the matter?"
As snowball chaos calls.

His friends all gather 'round,
With laughter in the air,
They build a snowy mound,
And play without a care.

One throws a flake away,
It lands on someone's nose,
They giggle and they sway,
In this chill, laughter grows.

So as they skate and slide,
They dance with pure delight,
With frosty laughter tied,
In a world of sparkling white.

Shards of Silence

The morning glows with glitter,
As squirrels hop with glee,
One stops to build a sitter,
Out of snow, just to see.

The frigid air does tickle,
While they munch on some seeds,
A snowman starts to giggle,
In frost, he plants some deeds.

Then here comes a bunny,
With a twinkle in his eye,
He jumps and makes it funny,
By giving snowballs a try.

They play until the night,
In silence, tales unfold,
With every frosty bite,
A story to be told.

Dances of the Cold

How the flakes twist and twirl,
Like dancing in a stream,
Each one a frosty pearl,
In a winter dream.

A snowman does a jig,
With carrot nose so bright,
He spins a little big,
Oh, what a silly sight!

Bunnies hop to the beat,
In their fluffy delight,
They can't help but repeat,
This dance in moon's light.

As the cold winds whistle,
They laugh under the stars,
Frost bites play like a missile,
As joy's their guiding cars.

Winter's Breath

The chill in the air is screaming,
As kids in mittens play,
Each breath looks like it's dreaming,
In this snowy ballet.

A misfit sock goes flying,
Ends up on someone's head,
Laughter starts multiplying,
As they end up misled.

A slide gives way to shivers,
As snowflakes talk and tease,
They trip and fall like rivers,
What fun in winter's freeze!

In snowball battles start,
Each throw is filled with cheer,
With a frosty little heart,
They conquer winter's sneer.

Ethereal Drift

Tiny daggers hang with glee,
Chilling where the sun can't see.
They giggle when the wind does sway,
A frosty dance in pure ballet.

A slip, a slide, oh what a mess!
An icy patch, a screaming dress.
The snowman waves with carrot grin,
Wishing he could come back in.

Frosty whispers in the night,
"Let's have snowball fights, alright?"
The world is draped in shimmering fun,
Until we slip and say, "I'm done!"

But each cold flake brings a cheer,
As snowmen gather, far and near.
In this chill, we find delight,
Laughing loud 'til morning light.

Glacial Echoes

In the yard, a white mound grows,
A fortress built with frozen flows.
The neighbor's dog makes quite the splash,
In snow that flies in a quick flash.

With every tumble, a squeal of joy,
We race downhill like a little boy.
"Oh no!" I shout, as I hit a tree,
"Now, that's one snowman, minus me!"

A snowball fight, oh what a sight,
I duck and weave, but lose the fight.
My friends are laughing, cheeks all red,
As I play dead—then take my spread.

The chilly laughter fills the air,
Winter's charm, beyond compare.
Underneath the frosty sky,
We build memories that never die.

Cascades of White

From rooftops, they tumble down like dreams,
Fluffy plumes burst at the seams.
With headgear on, I waddle out,
To join in all the shrieks and shouts.

Sleds zoom past like rockets bright,
Oh, what a lovely, snowy sight!
A plow arrives, oh how it rolls,
But I'm buried deep, losing my goals.

Snowflakes whisper as they crash,
And kids make snowmen as they splash.
But wait! An avalanche of kids in play,
Turns snowball fights into a fray.

As evening falls, we retreat inside,
With cups of cocoa, smiles spread wide.
Tomorrow comes with a fresh white glow,
Can't wait for this wild winter show!

The Secret Life of Cold

A chilly breeze with a sneaky grin,
Plans to tickle your nose and chin.
With every step, you stomp and shout,
"Why is winter taking me out?"

Fluffy blankets cover the ground,
As fashion statements come around.
With fuzzy hats and mittens tight,
We prance through drifts with pure delight.

Mischievous flakes swirl all around,
Snowmen plotting from snowy mound.
"Let's launch a snowball, aim for the head!"
And suddenly, the fun's widespread.

When night arrives with stars aglow,
The world is wrapped in a winter show.
With giggles 'til we shed a tear,
Oh, frosty joy, please stay all year!

Frozen Spikes at Dusk

Chilly daggers hang so near,
They wink and wiggle, oh so queer.
I tiptoe past, my toes a-twitch,
Avoiding every frozen hitch.

They drape the roof with a jagged grin,
A winter's jest, a frosty sin.
One topples down, it lands with flair,
I dodge and laugh, a cold affair!

Each spike a time bomb of frosty dread,
Making sure I watch my head.
I giggle loud as neighbors shout,
While dodging raindrops of ice about!

The twilight giggles in such a way,
With winter's tricks on full display.
Slippery, shiny—what a show,
I'll need a helmet, so off I go!

Whispering Winter Veils

The world's wrapped up in a frosty hug,
Each tree adorned with a winter mug.
They murmur secrets as I pass by,
But all I hear is their chilly sigh.

I trip on fluff, laugh like a child,
As winter's blanket turns me wild.
With snowflakes dancing, a wobbly waltz,
Their icy giggles are no one's fault!

The trees complain, "Oh, not today!"
"Why freeze our branches in such a way?"
I nod along, though I must confess,
Their winter fashion is quite a mess!

So I romp and roll with frozen cheer,
In this wintry land, where fun is near.
The veils of snow swirl and twirl,
Creating smiles in this frosty whirl!

Shards of Frost in Twilight

The evening gleams with sparkly strife,
Tiny crystals do a shimmery jive.
They catch the light, a disco dream,
As I bust a move—oh, how I gleam!

With each shatter, I jump in delight,
Making snow angels that giggle at night.
The shards give chase, a playful fray,
"Not on my watch!" I'll shout as I sway.

Frosty confetti dancing in line,
A slippery show, oh how divine!
They wink and tease as I float and slide,
This winter's playground—a frosty ride!

The sunsets giggle, a pastel glow,
As I tumble and wiggle through powdery snow.
Each frostbitten grin makes winter fun,
A gleeful shatter when day is done!

Crystal Teardrops from the Eaves

Round and round, the droplets hang,
Teardrops of laughter, winter's slang.
They glisten proudly like little jewels,
As I make faces, feeling like a fool!

Up above, they drip and sway,
"Catch me if you can!" they seem to say.
But with each splash, my wiggle goes,
A slippery slide, oh how it flows!

Down they fall, a shower of glee,
Transforming all into giggles for free.
The gutters chuckle, "Join the spree!"
As I leap, arms wide, and shout with glee!

Every drop is a little prank,
Just how many can this roof thank?
With dances now on the frosty floor,
Giggles resound, and I crave for more!

The Art of Winter's Caress

Frosty fingers wave hello,
As plump snowballs start to grow.
A waddle here, a tumble there,
We giggle hard without a care.

With scarves that dance and bob around,
We trip on sledge, fall to the ground.
Hot cocoa spills, sweet mess galore,
A winter art we can't ignore.

The frosty air, a biting tease,
Yet laughter flows with every breeze.
Snowmen wobble, hats fly high,
A comical cold, oh my, oh my!

Through fluffy drifts, we leap and play,
Ice cream headaches on display.
There's joy in every chilly act,
A frosty party, that's a fact!

Luminescent Ribbons of Ice

In the night, they twinkle bright,
Like stringy noodles caught in flight.
We dance beneath their glitzy show,
Slipping 'round like we're on a throw.

With shivers tickling at our toes,
We play dodgeball with falling snows.
Beware the pranks this season brings,
Silly falls and twice ripped things.

Jackets flapping, we look like birds,
Muffled laughter, awkward words.
A frisbee flies, it hits the tree,
Now where's the cookie, can't you see?

As glimmers wink from above our head,
We race and chase, full speed ahead.
Mom's hot pie, a welcome treat,
A winter feast is hard to beat!

Enchanted Chill Under Pale Light

The moon's a fridge, the stars are spry,
As snowflakes whirl like marshmallows fly.
We spin in circles, arms spread wide,
Falling down, our faces slide.

A frosty beast with a woolly coat,
Chased by laughter, on sleds we float.
Turned upside down in silver boots,
Hilarity reigns as everyone hoots!

The laughter peeks at chilly dawn,
As the frost-tipped world has withdrawn.
We seek snowmen with carrot noses,
Stumbling forth in winter's poses.

With bright balloons and giggling souls,
We take our part in winter goals.
This whimsical waltz, we can't resist,
In frosty wonder, joy persists!

Quickened Hearts in a Snowy Realm

Snowflakes whisper, what a sight,
As we prance like kids in flight.
With fluffy gear, we look so grand,
But trip on twirls, oh isn't it bland?

Chasing each other, round and round,
Finding surprises on the ground.
A scarf caught high, as if it screams,
We're rock stars in our frosty dreams.

The laugh that echoes, oh so bright,
Turning dull days into sheer delight.
Each tiny flake a joyful thrill,
Our winter adventures give hearts a thrill!

Through frozen steps, we march along,
In a world that hums a happy song.
Our hearts are quickened, spirits light,
In nature's riddle, we find delight!

Frosty Fingers on Nature's Sleeve

When winter's chill gives trees a shake,
Fingers frostbite, make the bark quake.
Squirrels in hats, they giggle in glee,
Fluffy tails bouncing, oh what a spree!

Frozen puddles, a slippery dance,
One wrong step, oh what a chance!
A tumble, a roll, some laughter's grace,
Nature's pranks! Oh, what a case!

Snowballs launched, a frosty fight,
With rosy cheeks, and dreams of flight.
Frosted tips on noses aglow,
Winter's joke, a splendid show!

So when you see the white blanket, dear,
Remember to smile, and share some cheer.
The cold may tease, but we'll always play,
In nature's game, let's frolic away!

Echoes of Snowfall's Embrace

Listen close, the snowflakes hum,
Singing songs, while winter's drum.
Whiskers twitch, little noses freeze,
Bouncing bunnies with frosty knees!

Moments freeze in frozen air,
A snowman grins, without a care.
Carrots misplaced, hats askew,
Oops! There goes the scarf, oh boo!

Noses run, while laughter flows,
Throw a snowball, right on your toes!
Slippery slopes, watch out below,
A tumble ensues, with a dash of woe!

In winter's grip, we find delight,
With giggles echoing through the night.
So raise your mug of hot cocoa high,
To snowflakes dancing from the sky!

Ethereal Layers of Shimmering White

Layers of fluff on the ground below,
Bounce like marshmallows, oh so slow.
Chubby cheeks and boots a-squish,
Creating snow angels, their frosty wish!

Mittens mismatched, a sight so grand,
Chasing winter's magic across the land.
But watch the path, it's slippery fun,
With giggles and squeals, let's run, run, run!

The sun peeked out, with a cheeky grin,
Melting dreams where the chaos began.
Puddles reflect, a funny sight,
Splash with joy, and feel the light!

Snowflakes twirl like dancers free,
Nature's jest, oh come with me!
Through sparkling drifts, let us glide,
In winter's laugh, we take our pride!

An Overture of Winter's Breath

Winter whispers, what a tease!
Puffing breath like frosty breeze.
Challenging folks to wear odd hats,
Pigeons dance, while snowmen chat!

A sled race down the hillside fast,
Bouncing like rubber, what a blast!
Comedic faceplants, and giggles abound,
As winter's gags push laughter around.

With cocoa spills and giggly slips,
Our winter story takes funny trips.
Each snowflake tells a punchline right,
In frosty fun, we find delight!

So bundle up, let's embrace the cold,
With brushes of laughter, our tales unfold.
For in this season's magical grip,
With merry hearts, let fellowship zip!

Shadows of Winter Light

The snow's a fluffy blanket, oh so deep,
A playground for squirrels, leaping with a beep.
Snowmen stand guard with carrot noses bold,
Their arms made of branches, looking quite old.

Hot cocoa spills from mugs, what a delight,
As marshmallows float like clouds in the night.
The wind sings a tune, tickling my face,
While I dance like a penguin, falling with grace.

The sun peeks through clouds, a sneaky spy,
Melting away snowflakes with a warm sigh.
I slip on the ice, like a cartoon show,
But laughter ensues as friends laugh and throw.

Children in snow forts, ready to attack,
With laughter and snowballs they'll never hold back.
Winter may chill, but it warms up the heart,
As memories form in this frosty art.

Shattered Chill

With a crunch beneath boots, I step on the street,
Noticing neighbors with mittens on their feet.
A snowball fight breaks out, oh what a sight,
As laughter erupts in the afternoon light.

The dog dashes past with a frisbee in tow,
Tumbling through drifts, putting on quite a show.
I join in the fray, sporting a grin,
Until I lose balance and tumble right in.

The icings of trees, like cakes in a bake,
You can't eat the frost, for goodness' sake!
As flakes gently flutter, they cover my hat,
I look like a snow-man, just like my cat.

Who knew winter's chill could bring such good cheer?
With snowflakes afloat, and friends gathered near.
Though I might be cold, my heart's feeling warm,
For in every snowball, there's joy as a norm.

Celestial Frost

In the still of the night, stars twinkle with glee,
While frosty white magic blankets the tree.
Fairies dance lightly on the tips of the leaves,
Mischievous whispers float down with the breeze.

A gentle chill settles, tickling my neck,
As I try to build castles—but what the heck?
My hands are too cold, they're icy and blue,
The walls start to sag; oh, what a to-do!

A snowflake lands softly right on my nose,
"It's a tiny white kiss!" I giggle and doze.
Chasing dreams 'til morning, I slip out of bed,
To find winter wonders awaiting instead.

With each plop of snow, I embrace my bright fate,
Who knew frozen magic could feel so first-rate?
Though winter can bite, it leads to delight,
As I twirl and I giggle, all wrapped up tight.

The Veil of Winter's Beauty

Under layers of white, the world wears a grin,
As feathers drift down, like a dozy cat kin.
The street lamps shine bright, like marshmallows aglow,
Illuminating paths where the silly kids go.

In boots that are squishy, I march like a train,
Through puddles of slush that go splat with a strain.
A snowman debates if to sport a top hat,
Or just keep it casual, like an old baseball cat.

The breeze tells a secret, it giggles and spins,
Around icy fences and past all the bins.
I wonder who makes every snowflake so unique,
They must have a big giggle from hiding all week.

So here's to the chill, and the silliness too,
With laughter and snow, it's a frosty to-do.
In winter's embrace, we twirl and we share,
For joy is found everywhere, even in the air!

The Glacial Embrace

Bundled up like a snowman, tight,
Hat on crooked, what a sight!
Falling fast, a slippery slide,
Squeals of laughter as we glide.

Hot cocoa spills on my new scarf,
Stuck up here, can't help but laugh.
Snowflakes dance like little jams,
And then I spot two frozen clams!

Kicked a snowball, hit a tree,
Oops! Now it's raining on me.
Chilled to the bone, I make a stand,
Waving at penguins on dry land!

Winter games go on all day,
Chasing doggos in white ballet.
Fluffy tails wagging with glee,
Snowmen giggle, just wait and see!

Enchanted Winter Dreams

With snowflakes swirling, all around,
I try to dance, but trip on ground.
The frost makes fairies, full of sass,
Sipping tea from a melted glass.

Building forts that collapse with ease,
While snowmen plot a big sneak tease.
One rolled away, right down the street,
Where kids shout, "Look! It's got two feet!"

Snowball fights, it's snow or shine,
The ground is covered, it feels divine.
When someone slips, oh what a show,
We laugh so hard, forget the cold snow.

In this wonderland, we feel so free,
With giggles echoing, just you and me.
Winter's magic makes us beam,
Rolled up in laughter, a chilly dream!

Beyond the Thaw

As the sun peeks out with a grin,
Snowflakes melt; let summer begin!
Bare patches show where we once played,
Now look! A puddle parade!

The winter hats now hang in shame,
They've seen too much; it's not the same.
Chasing ducks as they waddle through,
"Hey there, buddy, I'll race you too!"

Fluffy mittens shed their fluff,
The season teased, but it's not tough.
Rolling round in the slushy mess,
Just be careful, it's still a stress!

Our laughter echoes through the thaw,
The slip-slides come with such great awe.
Here's to snowflakes, here's to fun,
We'll dance with spring; the year's just begun!

A Chill in the Air

The air is crisp, it bites your nose,
Oh look! A set of jolly toes.
Frosty patterns on every pane,
I can't feel my fingers, what a pain!

Slicing through the frozen air,
A tumble here, a gentle scare.
Snowmen gossip while we play,
It's snow chaos, come join the fray!

Skating round on a patch of ice,
I spin and twirl, oh that's not nice.
Down I go, a graceful fall,
The snow's my cushion through it all!

Under blankets, hot drinks we'll share,
Giggles bubble with flair and care.
Chill in the air, but hearts are warm,
Winter's laughter is all the charm!

Frosted Dreams Beneath the Stars

In winter's night, the socks do slide,
Chasing snowballs, I take pride.
A snowman's hat? It's on my dog!
He's not impressed, he starts to jog.

Laughter echoes down the lane,
A snowflake lands upon my brain.
The chilly breeze is quite a tease,
It pulls my scarf with winter's ease.

I trip and slide upon the ground,
In frosty wonder, joy is found.
Each icy patch, a wild surprise,
I laugh so hard, I nearly cry.

Beneath the stars, we dance and spin,
With chilly cheeks, let games begin.
The night is full of frozen dreams,
As laughter flows like mountain streams.

Nature's Jewels: A Chilling Dance

Twinkling gems on branches cling,
Nature's bling, oh what a fling!
Each windy gust, a playful jab,
I wave hello to every slab.

Snowflakes swirl like paper planes,
We chase them down, forget our pains.
The crisp air bites, it's quite a thrill,
Yet here I am, sliding down hill.

Giggling squirrels with winter coats,
Dance around on wobblingboats.
Their acorn stash, I thought I'd find,
But it's buried deep, a sneaky bind.

Nature's gems in frosty air,
A winter's ball, we all can share.
With each cold snap, a howl of cheer,
Together we spread warmth and beer!

Silent Spheres of the Season

Round and fluffy, all around,
A snowball fight makes laughter sound.
Watch your back, my aim is true,
A frosty flake just hit your shoe.

The garden gnomes, they wear a frown,
With hats so thick, they can't sit down.
But sprinkle snow and watch them grin,
They join our fun, let games begin!

Winter's veil wraps the town tight,
Chasing shadows in the night.
In huddled groups, we laugh and squeal,
Those frozen feats, oh what a reel!

Silent spheres, we roll and tumble,
Soft white fluff that's sure to stumble.
As giggles rise beneath the moon,
The world is light, we're all in tune.

Frosty Fables on the Ground

A slippery tale beneath my feet,
Each cautious step, a rhythmic beat.
With every crunch, a story spins,
Of laughter shared and snowy wins.

The glaring sun gives way to shade,
Where frosty puddles start to fade.
But puddles beckon, a leap so bold,
If only I could stay, not cold!

Snow boots march like marching bands,
Thumping down like mighty hands.
The tales we weave in fluffy white,
Leave footprints bright, a silly sight.

Frosty fables on the ground,
Where every giggle can be found.
In chilly air, we play and play,
With joy that warms this winter day.

Winter's Palette

Snowflakes dance in chilly air,
A gust of wind gives them all a scare.
Hats fly off like kites gone wild,
While bundled kids can't help but smile.

Lumps of white roll down the lane,
A mountain of fun, but wait! What's this stain?
A snowman with a carrot nose,
Looks like he's struck a funny pose!

Snowballs fly with giggles galore,
Landing smack on the neighbor's door.
And with each throw, we start to see,
Mom's angry frown — but oh, it's glee!

So grab a sled and race downhill,
Spinning and tumbling, what a thrill!
While winter's fun may chill your toes,
The laughter lingers, goodness knows!

The Stillness of White

Blankets of white cover the ground,
In the quiet, funny sights abound.
A dog leaps up, a mistletoe snafu,
Ending up wrapped in a snowy goo!

Snowmen start to resemble blobs,
With funky styles from fashion mobs.
A scarf misplaced, a hat askew,
Is he a snowman or a frosty zoo?

Kids march forward with sleds in tow,
But a bump sends them squealing, 'Oh no!'
Wipeouts create a slapstick show,
As laughter echoes, their joy will grow.

Frosty fingers signal time to play,
As winter games sweep the blues away.
In the stillness, humor takes flight,
Making the cold feel warm and bright!

A Glacial Whisper

A chilly breeze, with secrets to tell,
As winter giggles under its spell.
Frost bites toes; oh, what a jest!
As boots go sliding, who knows the rest!

A snowball fight breaks out like war,
But laughter wins, with fun in store.
Sneeze and watch the snowflakes shake,
Funny how one sneeze can cause a quake!

Elves on trees with silly grins,
Frosted jokes that draw us in.
'You call that a snowman?' we'll tease,
While sipping cocoa, warm with ease!

Though winter seems to chill the air,
The giggles churn, beyond despair.
A glacial whisper brings us cheer,
As snowy antics persevere!

Mounds of Frost

Mountains of fluff fill the streets with glee,
As kids ski past with unbounded spree.
A rogue sled spins, oh what a sight!
Underneath the moon, everything feels right.

Frost-bitten cheeks and noses red,
Look at Dad; he's face-planted instead!
Snowmen smile with buttons round,
As if they're laughing at what they found.

Snow forts built with great precision,
But alas, all crumble in perfect decision.
What fun to toss and roll in this,
Winter's humor is hard to miss!

So bundle up, join in the fun,
Each frosty moment, a race to run.
Amidst mounds of frost, let joy not pause,
For winter's quirks deserve applause!

Ethereal White

The frosty flakes dance in the air,
Like tiny elves without a care.
They land on noses, hats, and shoes,
Creating chaos, laughter, and snooze.

The ground is dressed in fluffy pride,
A slippery slide that can't be denied.
We tumble and roll, giggles ignite,
In a fluffy world, oh what a sight!

The snowman stands with a crooked grin,
With buttons made from the last of the tin.
He's got a carrot, but that's not enough,
His arms made of twigs, oh so tough!

We build and break, oh what a thrill,
With snowballs flying, we can't sit still.
The fun erupts, laughter takes flight,
In this white wonderland, hearts feel light.

Cold Embrace

The world is wrapped in a chilly hug,
With jackets on, we're all snug as a bug.
We step outside, watch our breath billow,
It's a sneaky trap laid by winter's pillow.

Frosty mittens and bright red cheeks,
We prance in style, like funny freaks.
The cold may bite, but with it we play,
While landing face-first in soft, white ballet.

Sleds clatter down the old, steep hill,
We fly past trees with unspoken thrill.
Oh dear, the spinning and tumbling spree,
Coming to a stop—what fun it will be!

We shake off snow, like puppies so proud,
With laughter and joy bursting loud.
The cold embrace may be quite the tease,
But laughter warms hearts, such a winter breeze!

Frozen Remnants

The roof's dripped down, a sight so grand,
Like candy canes in a winter wonderland.
We chase the tricks of the slippery sheen,
While dodging the drips of old, frozen cream.

The car's a snow fortress, hidden from view,
As we wiggle and try to get through.
With boots like anchors, we wander about,
In search of lost treasures, there's no doubt!

Penguin-like waddles in thick, fluffy gear,
A race to the fence, but oh, what's near?
A pile of snow, the perfect invite,
To a splash of soft white, oh what a delight!

Onward we roll with snowballs in hand,
In this frozen kingdom, we take a stand.
A snowman's nose, but it's missing soon,
With laughter that echoes beneath the moon.

The Canvas of Ice

In a world where nature paints in white,
We slip and slide, what a comical sight!
With every step, we hope not to fall,
As laughter erupts, a magical call.

Snowflakes swirl like a wild confetti,
As we dodge and weave—oh, aren't we witty?
Chasing the glimmers like it's treasure,
In this frozen mirth, we find our pleasure.

Giant snow forts rise, a playful spree,
Where we launch volleys of snowballs with glee.
Each hit is a giggle, the thrill's never gone,
We're champions of winter, dusk 'til dawn!

The canvas of ice, every stroke a wild joy,
Turns winter blues into fun, life's a toy.
So let's dive right in, let the fun begin,
In a season that sparkles where giggles spin!

Frigid Glories

In winter's grasp, we slip and slide,
With snowballs flying far and wide.
A frosty breath, a chilly cheer,
We chuckle much, despite the fear.

The world is white, a blanket bright,
Yet we fall down, oh what a sight!
With every crunch beneath our feet,
We laugh aloud, can't feel the heat.

Hot cocoa spills, we splash and play,
The mug in hand won't go astray.
But with each sip, my fingers freeze,
A fuzzy mitt, oh how it teases!

Snowmen loom with carrots bright,
They wear our hats, oh what a fright!
Yet in their grins, we find delight,
Frosty friends in joy's own light.

The Frost's Lullaby

Snowflakes flutter, like tiny dancers,
While I stomp through with all the prancers.
My nose is red, my toes are cold,
Yet laughter rings, a joy untold.

A snow fort built, a fortress grand,
With ice bricks shaped by freezing hand.
We launch a blast, a chilly hit,
But down we go, with every bit!

The rooftops glisten like sugary treats,
While squirrels prepare their covert feats.
Who knew winter could bring such glee?
Amidst the cold, we're wild and free!

Shovels fly, as battles wane,
With snowflakes mixed in giggles' strain.
Each slip a tale of laughter's glow,
As winter's tale begins to flow.

Enveloping Silence

The world is hushed in blankets grey,
Where whispers melt, then drift away.
Yet each step crunches, loud and clear,
A symphony of frosty cheer.

Flaky blankets on cars we find,
My shovel gripes, it's in a bind.
But snowballs launch and giggles rise,
While frozen noses meet our eyes.

I think I saw that snowman grin,
As we tossed snow, our hearts within.
Yet one slipped down a snowy hill,
Chasing laughter, oh what a thrill!

The chilly air, it fills with fun,
As snowflakes dance, each one a pun.
In this stillness, joy takes part,
A winter's joke, a warming heart.

Hibernation of the Heart

As winter comes, we dream away,
Our blankets nestled, here we stay.
With cocoa warm and slippers snug,
We drift in dreams, all warm and dug.

The outside world is cold and bright,
But here I laugh, it feels just right.
With each howl of the winter breeze,
I share my snacks, I've got the keys!

The frostmay knock, yet still I sit,
Beneath the covers, snug and fit.
So let it snow, let tempests swirl,
My heart is warm, oh what a whirl!

Yet here I sit, with pie in hand,
While snowflakes fall, it's great and grand.
All winter long, let laughter start,
In comfy homes, a hibernated heart.

Shimmering Veils of the North Wind

In winter's grasp, they dangle down,
Like frozen chandeliers in town.
They sparkle bright, a gleaming sight,
But touch one quick and it takes flight!

The little ones laugh, they can't resist,
They reach for them, a gloved fist!
But whoops! They slip, a tumble, a roll,
A frosty hug for the playful soul.

With every twinkle, a jester's call,
The cold invites a slip and a fall.
Oh, winter's tricks, a playful tease,
A wobbly dance with chilly freeze.

Yet beneath the layers, the stories breathe,
Giggles and laughter in frosty wreaths.
For every slip, a tale unfolds,
In shimmering threads of winter's bolds.

Cascading Frost from Above

Oh, look at that! A chilly cascade,
A frosty waterfall, how it played!
The rooftops wear a snowy crown,
Like a fluffy hat for the sleepy town.

But watch your step, oh heed the ground,
For underneath lies a slippery mound.
With every hop and every leap,
A whoosh! A slide, a giggle to keep.

The snowflakes flutter like tiny gnomes,
Tricksters that dance far from their homes.
They swerve and twirl in a comic show,
Making winter's walk a game, you know?

So gather 'round, all young and old,
Embrace the fun, let the laughter mold.
For in the chill of the frosty swirl,
Life's better when you give it a whirl!

A Lullaby of Frozen Silence

In blankets soft, the world's asleep,
With whispers soft, the stillness creeps.
Yet wait, what's that? A giggle near!
The snow decided to bring some cheer.

It tumbles down in a fluffy cheer,
Covering all, bringing warmth near.
But peek out your door, and you may find,
A snowball fight of the quirky kind!

Listen close, oh hear the sound,
As frosty jesters dance around.
A silent lull, but watch the show,
The pranks unfold, a vibrant glow.

So while the night wears a frozen veil,
Adventure shimmies, it will unveil.
Laughter's chorus in winter's grace,
Turns silence into a merry race.

Stars Caught in a Chilly Embrace

The night is bright with a twinkling grin,
Frosty gems where the fun begins.
They gleam like laughter in the dark,
A chilly wink, a cheeky spark.

The trees play dress-up, all glitter and glow,
While chuckling shadows sneak to and fro.
They whisper tales of a playful freeze,
Of winter's charm and warm memories.

Oh, to run and jump with frosty delight,
With clanking boots that dance in the night.
Each flake a laugh, a pun of its own,
A snow world bursting with fun to be shown.

So tip your hat to the stars so bright,
In their chilly embrace, they spark our delight.
For even in cold, there's warmth we find,
In giggles and joy, so sweet and unconfined.

Whispers in Snow

The flakes come down, a fluffy beast,
A snowball fight, a frosty feast.
We chuck and laugh, a snowy blast,
With every throw, our troubles passed.

A sledding flop, right on my face,
My hat flies off, oh, what a race!
The snowman wobbles, one eye askew,
He seems to grin, and I'm stuck too.

Hot chocolate waits, oh, sweet divine,
But first more snowballs, I'll be fine!
The joy of winter, pure delight,
A silly game in chilly night.

So come and join, don't be too late,
Let's give the cold a run for fate!
The snow will melt, but laughs, my friend,
In frosty fun, we shall not end.

Frosted Fantasies

Snowflakes twirl, like tiny dancers,
They tickle noses, cause funny glances.
A snowman's hat looks like a broom,
What a strange sight, a frosty groom!

The dog hops high, he leaps and bounds,
But ends up stuck, rolling around!
A frozen rascal, he can't quite find,
The fastest way to peace of mind.

We build a fort, oh what a sight,
With walls so weak, no chance to fight.
One push, and down it goes with a thud,
We're all buried, what a snowy flood!

So gather friends, let laughter ring,
In chilly worlds where snowflakes sing.
For in this fun, let's be a part,
We'll treasure warmth inside our heart.

Glistening Dreams

The world is white, a sugar coat,
But watch your step, you might just float!
With every slip, we squeal and shout,
What was once grace is now in doubt!

A snow angel lies, with arms spread wide,
But mine looks more like I tripped and cried.
The wind it giggles, with frosty breath,
Encouraging jumps toward the cold death!

A snowball's thrown, oh, what a sight,
Right at my face, my moment of fright.
But laughter bounces, it's all in fun,
Here in the chill, we unite as one!

So grab your joys, let's play away,
With chilly winds, we'll dance and sway.
These frosted dreams bring glee, it's true,
In winter's grip, feel young anew!

Echoes of the Cold

The crunch of snow beneath my feet,
A symphony of winter's beat.
I toss a snowball, a perfect fling,
But hit a tree—oh, what a sting!

A chilly breeze, it nips my nose,
Each breath a cloud, in winter's prose.
I pull my scarf and shuffle close,
The birds just laugh, they know the most.

The sledding hill, it calls my name,
With every slide, it's all a game.
But with a spin, I lose my craft,
And tumble down, a frosty raft!

So gather near, embrace the cold,
For in the laughter, warmth we hold.
This snowy spell, let's make it bright,
In echoes loud, we chase the night.

Frosted Memories

The chilly winds usher in a time,
With laughter and snowballs, oh what a rhyme!
Falling, we tumble, then spring to our feet,
In this frosty wonder, oh joy can't be beat!

Hot chocolate flows as we bask in the freeze,
Wearing mittens that hug like the warmest of fleece.
We build snowy giants, all crazy and round,
And tell tales of snowflakes that dance without sound.

The hats on our heads are too big by a size,
While snowmen are dressed in the silliest ties.
With shovels like swords, we're knights on a quest,
Each snowdrift we conquer, we cheer and invest!

Memories frosted with giggles and cheer,
Oh, wintertime wonder, how we hold you dear!
In our moonlit kingdoms, where all things are bright,
We'll laugh through the cold, till we're out of sight!

Drifts of Diamond

In the morning light, sparkles take flight,
Glistening like jewels, oh what a sight!
We slip on the pavement, with laughs that ensue,
Each fall is a dance, in this glittering view.

Snowmen with noses so comically orange,
Wearing mustaches, so silly, oh please!
Friends dash about, doing backflips with cheer,
In this kingdom of fluff, all our worries disappear.

Chasing each other, our cheeks glow so bright,
As we carve out our paths in the shining white light.
With sleds made of boxes, we tumble and glide,
Through powdery pastures, all laughter and pride.

This season of joy, a whimsical gleam,
In a winter wonder, we laugh and we dream.
As the sun starts to set, we'll gather around,
And toast to the magic that knows no bounds!

Shimmering Cold

Hats tipped to one side, boots laced just right,
We frolic through drifts, oh what a delight!
With snowflakes a-twirling like dancers on stage,
We giggle and roll, acting out every age.

The cold seems inviting, a hug from the freeze,
As we munch on hot treats, oh yes, if you please!
With marshmallows floating like clouds in our cup,
We cheer for the season and never give up.

Stubby little fingers, with mittens too tight,
Sculpting bizarre creatures that fill us with fright.
They wobble and jostle, but bring us delight,
In this frosty fairytale, we're all set to write.

So here's to the winter, so crisp and so bold,
With stories and laughter, let's unleash and unfold!
We'll dance through the meadows, with joy on the way,
In shimmering wonder that brightens our day!

The Elegance of Winter

We glide and we slide, oh what a parade,
Through a blanket of white that nature's displayed.
There's elegance here, in each frosty breath,
With tippy-toed snowflakes that twirl to their death.

With laughter like fireworks, we tumble around,
Creating great memories, layered and sound.
A slip becomes giggles, we dance with such grace,
As we slide to a halt, with snow on our face!

Noses all rosy, like cherries so bright,
Our cheeks are a canvas, of winter delight.
We craft little angels, not meant to take flight,
In this frozen embrace, everything feels right.

So let's raise a toast, to snowflakes and cheer,
To the artful adventures that bring us near here!
In this merry season, where mishaps thrive well,
The elegance lingers, and hearts start to swell!

Whispering Frost

The frozen tears hang down from eaves,
Like nature's way of pulling sleeves.
A pop of joy, they catch the light,
But melt too soon, oh what a plight!

I slip and slide on crystal trails,
While laughing at my wobbly fails.
The chill brings shivers, what a show,
Yet here I am, still wanting snow!

Sometimes I swear, they've eyes that blink,
These chilly tricks that make me think.
They giggle softly as they sway,
And coax me into winter play!

With every fall, my face is red,
A frosty friend who won't be wed.
They tease with shimmies, sparkly pranks,
But oh, how I adore their flanks!

Crystalline Shards

Rooftops wear a shiny crown,
While puddles turn to frozen frown.
I dance around, avoiding slips,
On combo skates with joker flips!

Each twinkling dagger in the light,
Sends giggles flying, what a sight!
They sparkle here, they glimmer there,
But one wrong step—oh, what despair!

The ground is full of traps so sly,
That catch me off guard, oh my, oh my!
With each round fall, the laughter grows,
As snowflakes tangle in my clothes.

I swear they're plotting, just for fun,
As I perform my frosty run.
Yet underneath this playful guise,
I'll chase them till the sun will rise!

Winter's Silent Veil

A blanket of whimsy, soft and white,
Makes every step a comical fight.
I tumble, I giggle, oh what a mess,
While frost spins tales of winter's dress!

My nose is red, a bright beacon's light,
As I make snow angels with all my might.
They wink and wave, the snowflakes cheer,
While I battle snowdrifts with no fear!

Oh, how the frozen world does tease!
With icy whispers on the breeze.
A frosty dance, a clumsy twirl,
Each tumble is a gift, what a whirl!

And when at last the sun breaks free,
The laughing frost retreats from me.
But oh my heart, don't drift away,
For winter's joy will always stay!

The Art of Chill

The world's an artist painting white,
With every flake that takes its flight.
But catching snow is quite the trick,
I snatch at clouds, then fall, quite slick!

Nature giggles with every touch,
As fluffy puffs land, oh so much!
I leap and bound, a frosty jive,
With every fall, I feel alive!

With frosted breath, I blow a kiss,
To snowy hills I don't want to miss.
They wink and wave as I take a dive,
In this silly dance, I feel the vibe!

So here's to winters, wild and free,
Where every slip brings joy to me.
With laughter stitched into the thrill,
I master still the art of chill!

Hushed Snowfall

In a blanket of white, the world feels so calm,
Even the squirrels are wrapped up in charm.
A snowman with twigs, and a carrot for nose,
He wobbles and giggles, then suddenly doze.

The flakes dance around, soft whispers of frost,
A flurry of giggles, at no time is lost.
But watch for that slip, on the ice that's so slick,
It's a comedy show, as you tumble and kick.

Fragments of Ice

In the sun they do gleam, like slick little gremlins,
Yet underfoot's danger, oh, where are my hem-lyns?
With a waddle and shuffle, I make my grand stride,
But soon I'm a star, in a slip-up surprise glide.

The puddles reflect, look like glistening eyes,
Jon the dog jumps in, does a spectacular fly.
We laugh as he shakes, water flying about,
He looks like a monster, all furry and stout.

Glimmering Crystals

The tree branches are dressed, in diamonds they twinkle,
I spot one that glistens, oh look! It does crinkle.
And as it falls down, it lands on my nose,
I'm a snowflake magnet, oh dear, now it grows!

I chortle a lot, while I shake off the chill,
With hot cocoa in hand, it's a sweet little thrill.
The world's a big circus, with a slip and a shout,
A frosty parade, as winter comes out!

Enchanted by Winter

With mittens so fuzzy, I venture outside,
Where snowball fights happen, oh, let's take a ride!
But then there's a remnant, from my last friendly fling,
A snowball returns with a loud zany fling!

The flakes keep on falling, like feathers from heaven,
Yet the laughter it brings, is a total eleven.
In a world that is chilly, we find warmth inside,
With jokes like these, winter's here, come and bide!

Milton Keynes UK
Ingram Content Group UK Ltd.
UKHW022341171124
451242UK00007B/95

9 789916 945803